a Parent Guide *to* Prayer

Prayers of Our Faith

LOYOLA PRESS.
A JESUIT MINISTRY
Chicago

Finding **God**
Our response to God's gifts

ISBN-10: 0-8294-1900-4; ISBN-13: 978-0-8294-1900-9
Copyright © 2005 Loyola Press, Chicago, Illinois.

LOYOLA PRESS.
A JESUIT MINISTRY

3441 N. Ashland Avenue
Chicago, Illinois 60657
(800) 621-1008
www.loyolapress.com

11 12 13 14 Bang 10 9 8 7 6 5

Contents

PART THREE

Catholic Prayers and Devotions

Introduction

As a parent, you have a very special and unique relationship with your child. In order for this relationship to continue growing and developing, you and your child need to keep the lines of communication open. Without communication, relationships suffer.

God wants to be in communication with his children, just as any parent does. Our relationship with God, just as our other relationships, requires communication to remain healthy. Another word for this communication with God is prayer. God is always with us, inviting us to build a relationship with him through prayer.

Although this book contains many prayers, it is not primarily a prayer book. Rather, as the title states, it is a guide to prayer. We need guides for many things in life. Maps, tour guides, and study outlines provide direction in our everyday lives. This Parent Guide to Prayer provides direction for you and your child as you develop and maintain a relationship with God through a life of prayer.

This guide will provide you with direction as you accompany your child on a faith journey with the Lord.

To help your child develop a lifelong practice of prayer, it is important to set an example through your own prayer life. For this reason it is helpful for you to nourish and strengthen your own relationship with God through a life of prayer. Then you can more confidently assist your child as he or she enters into a deeper relationship with God through his or her own prayer life.

This guide is designed first and foremost to assist you as a parent in your own prayer life.

~ The Parent Guide to Prayer offers some ideas to help you understand what prayer is.

~ It provides you with practical information that can help you to find the types of prayer that you can practice by yourself as well as with your child. Many of these suggestions are based on an approach to prayer called the Ignatian method, named after the style of prayer taught by Saint Ignatius of Loyola.

~ It serves as a valuable and convenient source of traditional Catholic prayers and devotions.

PART ONE

Understanding Prayer

Keep It Simple

After dinner one night, Amy, a freshman at a Catholic high school, asked her dad, "Can you help me with an assignment? I'm supposed to write a prayer for religion class."

"Sure, I'll help," her dad replied, "but I'm not going to help you write the prayer. I'm going to teach you how to pray."

"OK, if you say so," responded Amy, looking somewhat puzzled but intrigued.

Dad explained, "The most important thing to remember about prayer is that God always makes the first move. God is always reaching out to us and inviting us to come to know him. When we pray, we are responding to God. Here are four ways we can respond to God in prayer. First, thank God for all the good things you have and for all the good that you've experienced recently. Second, tell God what your needs are. Third, tell God that you are sorry for the times that you haven't acted the way God would want you to. Finally, pray for the needs of others. If you remember these four things, you'll always be able to talk with God in prayer. The nice thing is, you don't always have to cover all four, and they don't have to be in a specific order. Just keep it simple."

Amy smiled as she took some notes. "That sounds easy," she replied. "Thanks."

Dad wished Amy well with her assignment and walked away thinking his work was done. Ten minutes later, however, Amy returned and said, "I understand what you told me, but I don't know how to put my thoughts into words. I'm not sure of what I would say."

Dad replied, "Just talk to God as if you were talking with a friend. If God walked into the room right now, and you wanted to begin by saying 'thank you,' what would you say 'thank you' for? Just write the way you would talk. Don't try to write poetry. Just keep it simple."

Amy responded, a surprised look on her face, "That's all there is to it? I thought it was more complicated than that."

"Talking with a friend is not complicated. Neither is talking to God," replied Dad.

Later, Amy returned with a prayer that she had written. Dad looked it over and congratulated her for doing such a fine job. "So, did you learn something about prayer from all of this?" he asked.

"Yeah . . . keep it simple!" she replied.

What Is Prayer?

As a parent you want your child to know that he or she can always come to you to talk or to ask for help. In the same way, God invites you to come to him with your thoughts and needs. The time that you spend aware of God's presence is called prayer. By taking time to become aware of God's presence, you can be open and talk with him about whatever is on your mind and in your heart.

You don't need special words to talk with God. As the dad told his daughter in the story, "Keep it simple." In fact a great teacher of prayer, Saint Ignatius of Loyola, taught that conversation with God should resemble the way that one friend speaks with another; God knows you and understands. He listens to you because he loves you as a parent loves a child.

Prayer is more than simply talking with God, however. In Saint Paul's first letter to the Thessalonians, he advises us to "pray constantly" (1 Thessalonians 5:17). If prayer were simply understood as "talking to God," then it might seem as though Saint Paul gave us the impossible task of talking constantly to God. If we understand prayer as the time we spend aware of God's presence, however, it is indeed possible to pray constantly because God is with us at all times.

Prayer is a gift from God. When you respond by accepting this gift, prayer nourishes your personal relationship with God and does the same for your child. Through daily prayer you develop the practice of acknowledging God's presence in every aspect of your life.

Praying in Many Ways

Today you have so many ways to communicate with others. You can send and receive e-mails, faxes, phone calls, text messages, and letters, or, you can do it the old-fashioned way and talk to someone face to face! You can communicate with God in many ways as well. Because prayer is vital to anyone's relationship with God, the Church teaches us to pray often and in many ways.

There is no one way to pray. Just as you relate in various ways to your friends, you relate in many ways to God. You can use different ways of praying at different times. The important thing is to pray regularly and in a way that you are comfortable with.

For many Catholics, traditional prayers and Sunday Mass are the most familiar forms of prayer. The traditional prayers of our Catholic heritage are a good starting point as are the traditional prayer moments such as morning prayer, evening prayer, and grace before and after meals. Likewise, Sunday Mass is a form of communal prayer that is at the very heart of Catholic prayer life. In addition to these forms of prayer, the Church also teaches a wide variety of ways to pray and prayer forms.

Ways to Pray

You can pray alone. Just as you talk with your best friends and share what is going on in your life, so too can you talk to God. Just as you listen to your friends, so too can you listen to God. You can pray to God in your own words. You can pray with others in communal prayer. When you pray with others, you may rely on the traditional prayers that unite us in our Catholic way of life. You can pray silently or aloud. You can pray using different postures and gestures: genuflecting, kneeling, standing, bowing, folding your hands, and praying the Sign of the Cross. There are many options to choose from. You can pray anytime—while you are relaxing, working, walking, or playing.

Forms of Prayer

Sometimes you might bless or adore God for his greatness (prayer of blessing and adoration). Other times you might ask God for something for yourself, asking God's forgiveness for your sins or asking him to grant your needs (prayer of petition). Sometimes you might pray for others (prayers of intercession). When you ask on behalf of another, you pray as Jesus did when he interceded with God for all of us in the words of the Lord's Prayer. You might also thank God in prayer for his gifts to you (prayer of thanksgiving). Finally, you might give praise to God (prayer of praise), recognizing that God is God and giving him glory for his being.

Reflective Prayer—Meditation

With so many distractions in your busy life, it can be difficult to remain focused on God's presence. To help you focus on God's presence, the Church teaches meditation, which is also known as reflective prayer. To meditate is to reflect on or think about God. When we meditate, we keep our attention and focus on God so that we can recognize his presence in our daily lives and respond to what he is asking of us. Scripture, prayer books, or religious images can help you concentrate. They can also spark your imagination so that you can recognize God's presence in your daily life and respond to what he's asking of you. Meditation leads you to a conversation with God and to placing yourself in his presence where you can listen to him speak to you. You can enter into God's sacred time and space and know that he is with you at all times and wherever you are.

Resting in God's Presence—Contemplation

Some of the most cherished moments you share with your child are when you simply hold him or her in your arms and no words need to be spoken. You can enjoy this same experience with God. When you rest quietly in God's presence, you engage in the form of prayer called contemplation. In contemplation you can spend time with God in silence, being aware that he is with you. Contemplation might be better understood by thinking of how you feel when you look at a beautiful sunset or a treasured possession. You are conscious of its meaning, but your response is wordless. In the same way, when you experience God, you feel his love and wait for him to speak to you in his own way. The key is to make time to relax and be attentive to God's presence, to seek union with God who loves you.

Making Prayer a Practice—
For Yourself and for Your Family

As enthusiastically as you respond to a close friend's invitation to spend time together, you can respond to God's invitation to share yourself with him in prayer. God is with you always and everywhere; you can pray whenever you want and wherever you are. If you pray daily, whatever kind of prayer you like, you will build the practice of prayer for your own life and set an example for your child to follow.

How do you build a practice into your life? We build practices simply by doing something over and over again until they become second nature. The regularity of your prayer is more important than the length of your prayers. Setting aside a certain time in your day and a special place where others will respect your space and silence will encourage daily prayer. Prayer is not a chore that you have to complete. Rather it is a gift—an opportunity to bask in the presence of God. The practice of prayer will be easier to build if you approach it as time set aside for indulging in God's abundant grace as opposed to completing a required task.

The practice of prayer is also easier to build if you remind yourself that you are the one who needs prayer, not God. Like a plant that needs sunshine and water, you need the spiritual enrichment that comes from a life of prayer.

Designating a special time and place is also helpful for building the practice of prayer. Think of this place as your oasis or your sacred space. Make this space special by placing a Bible, a candle, and a crucifix or other sacred image on a small table near wherever you plan to make yourself comfortable for prayer.

Finally, build the practice of prayer by removing the pressure of trying to impress God with the right words. You do not have to prove yourself to God. God is simply looking for you to seek him so that you can come to recognize the gift of grace that he offers you. Just be present to God and allow him to do the "work" of prayer.

Children learn from their parents. One of the best practices we can teach our children is the practice of prayer. The family is the first place where children learn to pray, to worship God, to love, to forgive, and to work together.

Because of this special role that the family plays in forming the faith of children, Christianity thinks of the family as the domestic church. This description suggests that the Christian family is a community of grace and prayer—a "school" of human virtues and charity.

Significant family events, both joyful and sad, can be occasions for family prayer: a birthday, the birth of a new baby, an illness in the family, or the loss of a pet. How often you pray together as a family is not as important as the regularity with which you pray together. The important thing is to make the prayers your own. Allow your prayers to reflect what's important to you and what concerns you and your family. Traditional prayers can be combined with spontaneous prayer of your own, thanking God for various blessings, asking God's blessings on family members or on the events of the day, or asking for help to face challenges.

Praying as a family not only will draw you closer as a family but will also emphasize to your child the importance of being constantly aware of God's presence. A family commitment to prayer will help your child develop a lifelong habit of prayer.

Jesus said, "For where two or three are gathered together in my name, there am I in the midst of them" (Matthew 18:20). When we gather as a family in prayer, we draw attention to the presence of Jesus in the home. Praying together strengthens the bonds of family life. The more a family community gathers in prayer, the more children will see prayer as an important part of their lives.

PART TWO

Learning How to Pray

Lord, Teach Us to Pray

In the Gospel of Luke, we learn that Jesus' disciples came to him one day and said, "Lord, teach us to pray" (Luke 11:1). Jesus responded by teaching them what we today call the Our Father or the Lord's Prayer. The powerful words of this traditional prayer, as expressed in Matthew 6:9–13, have been handed on from generation to generation.

It is important to know that not only was Jesus teaching words for prayer with the Our Father, he was also teaching an attitude for prayer. In teaching the words of this prayer, Jesus teaches us to approach God as we would approach someone with whom we have an intimate relationship. Jesus teaches us to approach God in prayer with an attitude of praise and gratitude, trust and surrender, and of sincere sorrow for our wrongdoings. With this attitude in mind, we can respond to God in prayer in a variety of ways.

Traditional Prayers

It's always good to start with what we are most familiar. Most likely you learned traditional prayers in your childhood: the Our Father, the Hail Mary, grace before and after meals, hymns, and so on. These prayers are like family heirlooms, passed from generation to generation. When you pray with these words, you join your voice to the countless voices past and present that have prayed and continue to pray them to respond to God's call to grow in our relationship with him. Traditional prayers are extremely helpful when we cannot find our own words to pray. As with all prayer, traditional prayers can be used at any time. You may want to use traditional prayers to help you begin and end your day as well as to mark significant moments in your day such as meals, restful pauses, or moments of solitude. To help you recall the words of these traditional prayers, this Parent Guide to Prayer contains a treasury of traditional Catholic prayers and devotions (page 31).

With Your Child

The last part of this book (beginning on page 31) will assist you in your efforts to help your child take to heart the words of traditional Catholic prayers and devotions. Use this section to talk with your child about and review the prayers he or she is learning in the Finding God sessions. Help your child learn not only the words but also the meaning of these traditional prayers and devotions. The Raising Faith-Filled Kids parent pages that your child brings home regularly will alert you to the various prayers that he or she is learning.

Praying in Your Own Words

Praying in your own words may seem somewhat intimidating at first. If you remember to "keep it simple" however and talk to God as though you were talking to a friend, you can pray in your own words at any time and place. Don't get hung up on trying to use long, fancy words. Talk to God about your hopes, fears, joys, dreams, desires, challenges, and worries. Remember the advice the dad gave to his daughter in the story from Part One of this guide:

~ thank God for all the good things you have and for all the good that you've experienced recently;

~ tell God what your needs are;

~ tell God that you are sorry for the times that you haven't acted the way he would want you to;

~ pray for the needs of others.

With Your Child

Praying in your own words can be done silently or aloud. By occasionally praying in your own words out loud, you can teach your child this valuable habit. Encourage your child to stop while you are outside enjoying nature together to thank God for the beautiful flowers, the sunny day, the songbirds in the trees, or other aspects of creation. When beginning a school project together, include God by asking his help to do a good job.

The Mass

Of all the ways of praying as a Catholic, you are probably most familiar with the Mass. Yes, the Mass is a form of prayer. In fact it is the most important way that we pray as Catholics because it brings us together as a community to hear God's Word and to receive Jesus Christ in the Eucharist.

Because prayer is the time we spend aware of God's presence, there is no more powerful way to pray than the Mass. We sometimes forget that the Mass is a form of prayer . . . something we need to consciously and actively participate in rather than passively attend. Regardless of whether the music, preaching, and environment are of the highest quality or leave something to be desired, the fact remains that the Mass is an opportunity to hear God's invitation and to respond in thanksgiving for the many ways that he fills our lives with blessings.

With Your Child

Help your child to recognize that the Mass is the most important way that Catholics pray. Going to Mass with your child is one of the greatest gifts you can offer because you are bringing him or her to encounter Christ in the most profound way possible—in the Eucharist. Help your child to pray by arriving early, by taking time to quiet yourselves, and by participating in the songs and prayers of the Mass. Work together to learn some familiar hymns so that he or she can more fully participate in the Mass.

Prayerfully Reviewing Your Day

Part of the rich tradition of the Catholic Church is recognizing the need to reflect on the day's activities—to remember God's invitation and our response or lack of response. Saint Ignatius of Loyola developed a simple method by which you can review each day in a way that will help you grow in self-understanding and free you to follow God's will. This practice is often called the Daily Examen. Many people choose to practice this prayerful review of their day before going to bed at night by following the five steps below.

Stillness: Recalling God's Presence

Relax in God's presence in your favorite prayer place and posture. Be aware of how God shows his love for you in all his gifts to you. Be thankful as you think of God the Father's love, the love of his Son Jesus, and the guidance of the Holy Spirit. Ask the Holy Spirit to come into your heart and to help you to look honestly at your actions this day and how you have responded in different situations. With the Spirit's inspiration you can recognize what draws you close to God as well as what pulls you away from God.

Gratitude: Expressing Thankfulness

Review your day and give thanks to God for his gifts. Try not to choose what to be thankful for but rather to see what springs to mind as you reflect. Think of the concrete details of your day—the aroma of coffee brewing, a smile from a co-worker, or a beautiful rainbow. Recall the gifts that God has given you that you can share with others—your ability to help in a crisis, your sense of humor, or your patience with children. Pause and express your gratitude to the Father, the Son, and the Holy Spirit.

Reflection: Looking Back on Your Day

Again review the events of the day and notice how you acted in the many situations in which you found yourself. Recall your feelings and motives to see whether you considered all of the possibilities and freely followed God's will. Ask yourself when you were conscious of God's presence. Think about opportunities you had to grow in faith, hope, and charity. When we think about why we did or did not take advantage of these opportunities, we can become aware of how we might change our actions in the future. Be grateful for the occasions when you freely chose a course to help others. Perhaps you let a shopper with a small order go ahead of you in line or did not join in a conversation critical of a co-worker. These are examples of responding freely as God wants us to. When we reflect on the times we did or didn't act with God's grace, we can be more sensitive to developing habits of positive responses.

Sorrow: Asking for Forgiveness

After you have asked for the Holy Spirit's guidance in recalling and reflecting on the actions of your day, spend time talking with God or Jesus. Express sorrow for the times you failed to follow his direction and ask him to be with you the next time you encounter a similar situation. Give thanks to God for the grace that enabled you to follow his will freely. Feel the sorrow and gratitude in your heart as you converse with God.

Hopefulness: Resolving to Grow

Ask God to help you as you look forward to a new day tomorrow. Resolve to cooperate and trust in the loving guidance of the Father, the Son, and the Holy Spirit. Conclude the day's prayerful review with the Lord's Prayer.

By prayerfully reviewing your day, you will experience the difference it can make in the way you live. If you make a habit of practicing the Daily Examen, you will grow closer to God in your thoughts and deeds and will be free to choose to follow him.

With Your Child

The practice of reviewing your day (Daily Examen) is a wonderful gift to share with your child. The simplicity of the Examen makes it a perfect fit for the prayer life of a child. With a young child, you can talk through the steps, inviting him or her to say thank you to God for good things; to think about the day and how he or she moved closer to God or farther away from God; to say "I'm sorry" for the times he or she did not act as God wishes; and to ask for God's help in growing closer to him tomorrow. With an older child, teaching this formula can aid the transition from the way he or she prayed as a little child into the way he or she can pray as a young adult.

Reflective Prayer

Despite the fact that family life can be hectic at times, you don't need to go to a monastery or search for a deserted place in the woods to pray. You simply need to make a transition of focus so that you can become more in tune with God's presence in your activities. In reflective prayer, also known as meditation, you can use your mind and imagination to engage in prayerful conversation with God and to recognize his presence in your daily life. Reflective prayer involves the following simple steps:

Find a quiet place where you can be alone for 10 or 15 minutes. Assume a comfortable position and, if you wish, close your eyes or focus on a religious picture or a lighted candle. If you wish, play soft background music to help establish a prayerful mood. Become aware of God's presence and ask the Holy Spirit to guide your reflection.

Take 2 or 3 minutes to practice rhythmic breathing—counting to three slowly and silently while breathing in and counting slowly to five while breathing out—to help you concentrate. If you become distracted, return to concentrating on your breathing and let the distractions go by so that you can turn your heart back to God. Likewise, you can choose a special word or phrase, such as Jesus or My Lord and My God, and repeat it when you are distracted to bring your attention back to God's presence.

Prayerfully read a brief passage from Scripture that you have selected for inspiration. If the passage is a Gospel story, imagine yourself as a participant in the story. In your imagination use your five senses to enter a setting in which you can talk with Jesus and listen to him speak to you. You can respond to what Jesus is saying or doing in the story, or you can simply talk about something that has happened to you recently or about a forthcoming event in your life.

In addition to using Scripture in your reflection, you can also use writings from or about the saints as well as other inspirational literature or prayer books. Likewise, you can choose to concentrate on a sacred object such as a crucifix or reflect on a sacred image such as an icon of Jesus or a favorite saint. Take this time to talk to God as you would to a friend.

End your reflection with one or two minutes of contemplation, time to rest silently in God's presence. As adults we come to recognize more and more that God speaks to us using the language of silence. Take a few moments at the end of your reflection to enter into a few silent moments with God.

With Your Child

Reflective prayer plays an important role in the Finding God program that your child is participating in. A reflective prayer related to the theme of the session helps children use their imaginations, along with thought, emotion, and desire to enter into sacred time and space.

You can help your child's prayer life by taking the time to pray reflectively together. Reflective prayer can be a wonderful bedtime prayer. You can use the same steps outlined above, helping your child to get comfortable, experience some quiet, and then imagine himself or herself in a Bible story. Together imagine the setting and the characters. Ask questions of your child, such as who he or she would like to be in the story and what he or she would say to Jesus. Your guidance with questions that involve all of the senses—What can you see? What sounds do you hear? What can you feel?— will help your child to become involved in the scene. Guide your child in a conversation with Jesus and in a quiet time to listen to what Jesus wants to reveal.

Taking time for reflective prayer in your own life will allow you to help your child develop the same habits. Through reflective prayer you and your child can recognize God's presence in your daily lives.

PART THREE

Catholic Prayers and Devotions

Family Heirlooms

Although you can pray with any words that come to mind, you may find that choosing your own words is sometimes difficult. At those times, you can use traditional prayers. Likewise, when you pray communally, you will find that using traditional prayers will connect you to those with whom you are praying as well as to those who have used these prayers down through the ages.

One of the ways we sustain the "memory" of the Church is through the memorization of traditional prayers, such as those that follow. When we memorize prayers, we take them to heart, meaning that we not only learn the words but also try to understand and live them. These prayers are like family heirlooms, passed on from generation to generation, linking us to the basic truths of our faith, supporting personal prayer, and allowing groups of people to unite their minds, hearts, and voices.

Children like to be grown-up enough to participate in the communal prayers of their own families and the family of the Church. Review and pray the traditional prayers with your child to help him or her take them to heart. Discuss the meaning of a prayer, phrase by phrase, as you pray it together. If your child is able to read the prayer you are praying, look together at the words as you pray them. Seeing and hearing the words can help your child to become familiar with the prayer. Talk with your child about the meaning of the prayer first; focusing on the meaning will help your child to recall the words of the prayer. When your child is familiar with the prayer, pray it aloud yourself and pause for him or her to fill in words or phrases. Each time you do this, have your child fill in more and more words.

Young children might be helped by drawing pictures to represent parts of a prayer. The pictures can be a reminder of the sequence of the prayer. Making up ways of acting out a prayer might also help young children to associate words and meaning. Reciting a prayer aloud with expression will help fix the prayer in your child's memory.

All of the prayers that follow are introduced to children at various grade levels in Finding God. Talk with your child about the prayers that are being introduced in his or her sessions. These conversations are the perfect opportunity to help your child practice the particular prayer that he or she is learning and to explain to you the meaning of the prayer. This kind of sharing remains with us throughout our lives as we associate them with the prayer and with the people in our lives.

Our Catholic heritage is rich in tradition. With your help your child will share in this heritage and will grow in a relationship with God through a life of prayer.

Sign of the Cross

In the name of the Father,

and of the Son,

and of the Holy Spirit.

Amen.

Glory Be to the Father

Glory be to the Father,

and to the Son,

and to the Holy Spirit.

As it was in the beginning,

is now, and ever shall be,

world without end.

Amen.

Lord's Prayer

Our Father, who art in heaven,

hallowed be thy name;

thy kingdom come,

thy will be done

on earth as it is in heaven.

Give us this day our daily bread,

and forgive us our trespasses,

as we forgive those who trespass against us;

and lead us not into temptation,

but deliver us from evil.

Amen.

Hail Mary

Hail Mary, full of grace,

the Lord is with you.

Blessed are you among women,

and blessed is the fruit of your womb, Jesus.

Holy Mary, Mother of God,

pray for us sinners,

now and at the hour of our death.

Amen.

Prayer to My Guardian Angel

Angel of God, my guardian dear,

to whom God's love commits me here,

ever this day be at my side,

to light and guard, to rule and guide.

Amen.

Morning Offering

My God, I offer you my prayers,

works, joys and sufferings of this day

in union with the holy sacrifice of the Mass throughout the world.

I offer them for all the intentions of your Son's Sacred Heart,

for the salvation of souls, reparation for sin,

and the reunion of Christians.

Amen.

Morning Prayer

God, our Father,

I offer you today

all that I think and do and say.

I offer it with what was done on earth

by Jesus Christ, your Son.

Amen.

Evening Prayer

God, our Father, this day is done.

We ask you and Jesus Christ, your Son,

that with the Spirit, our welcome guest,

you guard our sleep and bless our rest.

Amen.

Prayer Before Meals

Bless us, O Lord, and these your gifts

which we are about to receive from your goodness.

Through Christ our Lord.

Amen.

Prayer After Meals

We give you thanks

for all your gifts,

almighty God,

living and reigning

now and for ever.

Amen.

Peace Prayer of Saint Francis

Lord, make me an instrument of your peace:

where there is hatred, let me sow love;

where there is injury, pardon;

where there is doubt, faith;

where there is despair, hope;

where there is darkness, light;

where there is sadness, joy.

O divine Master, grant that I may not so much seek

to be consoled as to console,

to be understood as to understand,

to be loved as to love.

For it is in giving that we receive,

it is in pardoning that we are pardoned,

it is in dying that we are born to eternal life.

Amen.

Prayers of Saint Ignatius of Loyola

Suscipe

Take, Lord, and receive all my liberty,

my memory, my understanding

and my entire will,

All I have and call my own.

You have given all to me.

To you, Lord, I return it.

Everything is yours; do with it what you will.

Give me only your love and your grace,

That is enough for me.

Prayer for Generosity

Eternal Word, only begotten Son of God,

Teach me true generosity.

Teach me to serve you as you deserve.

To give without counting the cost,

To fight heedless of wounds,

To labor without seeking rest,

To sacrifice myself without thought of any reward

Save the knowledge that I have done your will. Amen.

Prayer to the Holy Spirit

Come, Holy Spirit, fill the hearts of your faithful.

And kindle in them the fire of your love.

Send forth your Spirit and they shall be created.

And you will renew the face of the earth.

Lord,

by the light of the Holy Spirit

you have taught the hearts of your faithful.

In the same Spirit

help us to relish what is right

and always rejoice in your consolation.

We ask this through Christ our Lord.

Amen.

Apostles' Creed

I believe in God,

the Father almighty,

Creator of heaven and earth,

and in Jesus Christ, his only Son, our Lord,

who was conceived by the Holy Spirit,

born of the Virgin Mary,

suffered under Pontius Pilate,

was crucified, died and was buried;

he descended into hell;

on the third day he rose again from the dead;

he ascended into heaven,

and is seated at the right hand of God the Father almighty;

from there he will come to judge the living and the dead.

I believe in the Holy Spirit,

the holy catholic Church,

the communion of saints,

the forgiveness of sins,

the resurrection of the body,

and life everlasting. Amen.

Nicene Creed

I believe in one God,

the Father almighty,

maker of heaven and earth,

of all things visible and invisible.

I believe in one Lord Jesus Christ,

the Only Begotten Son of God,

born of the Father before all ages.

God from God, Light from Light,

true God from true God,

begotten, not made, consubstantial with the Father;

through him all things were made.

For us men and for our salvation

he came down from heaven,

and by the Holy Spirit was incarnate of the Virgin Mary,

and became man.

For our sake he was crucified under Pontius Pilate,

he suffered death and was buried,

and rose again on the third day

in accordance with the Scriptures.

He ascended into heaven

and is seated at the right hand of the Father.

He will come again in glory

to judge the living and the dead

and his kingdom will have no end.

I believe in the Holy Spirit, the Lord, the giver of life,

who proceeds from the Father and the Son,

who with the Father and the Son is adored and glorified,

who has spoken through the prophets.

I believe in one, holy, catholic and apostolic Church.

I confess one Baptism for the forgiveness of sins

and I look forward to the resurrection of the dead

and the life of the world to come. Amen.

Act of Contrition

My God,

I am sorry for my sins with all my heart.

In choosing to do wrong

and failing to do good,

I have sinned against you

whom I should love above all things.

I firmly intend, with your help,

to do penance,

to sin no more,

and to avoid whatever leads me to sin.

Our Savior Jesus Christ

suffered and died for us.

In his name, my God, have mercy.

Act of Faith, Hope, and Love

Jesus, I believe in you.

Jesus, I hope in you.

Jesus, I love you.

Act of Faith

O my God, I firmly believe that you are one God

in three divine Persons, Father, Son, and Holy Spirit.

I believe that your divine Son became man and died for our sins,

and that he will come to judge the living and the dead.

I believe these and all the truths

which the holy Catholic Church teaches,

because you have revealed them,

who can neither deceive nor be deceived. Amen.

Act of Hope

O my God, relying on your infinite mercy and promises,

I hope to obtain pardon of my sins, the help of your grace,

and life everlasting, through the merits of Jesus Christ,

my Lord and Redeemer. Amen.

Act of Love

O my God, I love you above all things

with my whole heart and soul, because you are all good

and worthy of all my love.

I love my neighbor as myself for the love of you.

I forgive all who have injured me

and I ask pardon of those whom I have injured. Amen.

Prayer for Vocations

God, in Baptism you called me by name

and made me a member of your people, the Church.

Help all your people to know their vocation in life,

and to respond by living a life of holiness.

For your greater glory and for the service of your people,

raise up dedicated and generous leaders who will serve as sisters,

priests, brothers, deacons, and lay ministers.

Send your Spirit to guide and strengthen me that I may serve

your people following the example of your Son, Jesus Christ,

in whose name I offer this prayer.

Amen.

Hail, Holy Queen

Hail, holy Queen, Mother of mercy,

hail, our life, our sweetness, and our hope.

To you we cry, the children of Eve;

to you we send up our sighs,

mourning and weeping in this land of exile.

Turn, then, most gracious advocate,

your eyes of mercy toward us;

lead us home at last

and show us the blessed fruit of your womb, Jesus:

O clement, O loving, O sweet Virgin Mary.

Magnificat

My soul proclaims the greatness of the Lord,

my spirit rejoices in God my Savior;

for he has looked with favor on his lowly servant.

From this day all generations will call me blessed:

the Almighty has done great things for me,

and holy is his Name.

He has mercy on those who fear him

in every generation.

He has shown the strength of his arm,

he has scattered the proud in their conceit.

He has cast down the mighty from their thrones,

and has lifted up the lowly.

He has filled the hungry with good things,

and the rich he has sent away empty.

He has come to the help of his servant Israel

for he has remembered his promise of mercy,

the promise he made to our fathers,

to Abraham and his children for ever.

Memorare

Remember, most loving Virgin Mary,

never was it heard

that anyone who turned to you for help

was left unaided.

Inspired by this confidence,

though burdened by my sins,

I run to your protection

for you are my mother.

Mother of the Word of God,

do not despise my words of pleading

but be merciful and hear my prayer.

Amen.

The Rosary

The Rosary is a treasured prayer of the Catholic Church that helps us to understand the mystery of Christ's life and to pray to him through Mary. When we pray the Rosary, the words of the prayers unite with the images that we associate with the special events, or mysteries, in the lives of Jesus and Mary. We honor Mary by sharing in the life of her Son.

Centuries ago people used objects such as rocks and sticks to keep track of the numbers of prayers they had recited. Early monks prayed the 150 psalms and often used beads or knotted ropes to count them. Later the Lord's Prayer or the Hail Mary was often recited in place of the psalms.

The Rosary as we know it today probably began with Saint Dominic. He is said to have received it from the Blessed Mother and its practice evolved over the years. The word *rosary* means "crown of roses," so some people consider praying the Rosary as a spiritual bouquet or a crown of roses offered to Mary.

Throughout Church history the popes have recommended that we pray the Rosary with our family. By reflecting on the mysteries in the life of Christ, we appreciate more deeply his love for us and share our understanding of that love with our children.

Talk to your child about the Rosary and share your own experiences. Provide your child with his or her own rosary to hold as you show him or her the parts and talk about the prayers. If possible gather your family in a special place to pray the Rosary together. If very young children are involved, you might pray one mystery a day. Possibly begin by reading about the mystery from a children's Bible or storybook. Older children might be encouraged to take turns leading the family Rosary.

How to Pray the Rosary

A rosary consists of a string of beads and a crucifix. To pray the Rosary, we hold the crucifix in our hands as we pray the Sign of the Cross and the Apostles' Creed.

Following the crucifix there is a single bead, a set of three beads, and another single bead. We pray the Lord's Prayer as we hold the first single bead and a Hail Mary at each bead in the set of three that follows. Then we pray the Glory Be to the Father. On the next single bead we think about the first mystery and pray the Lord's Prayer.

There are five decades, or sets of ten beads. We pray a Hail Mary on each bead of a decade as we reflect on a particular mystery in the lives of Jesus and Mary. The Glory Be to the Father is prayed at the end of each set. Between decades is a single bead on which we think about the next mystery and pray the Lord's Prayer. We end by holding the crucifix as we pray the Sign of the Cross.

One way to pray the Rosary as a family (or in any group), is to have one person take the role of leader. The leader prays the first part of each prayer followed by the other group members praying the last part of each prayer:

Leader	Others
Our Father,	Give us this day
Hail Mary,	Holy Mary, Mother of God,
Glory be to the Father,	As it was in the beginning,

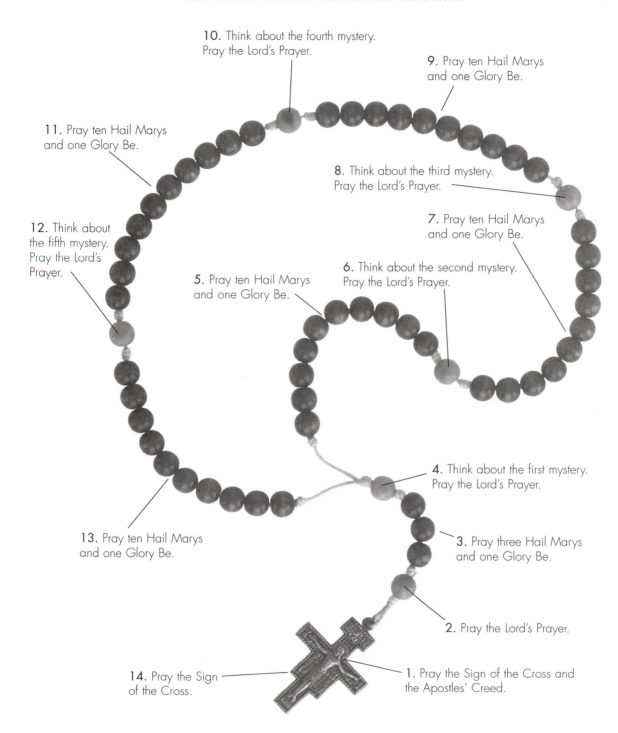

10. Think about the fourth mystery. Pray the Lord's Prayer.

9. Pray ten Hail Marys and one Glory Be.

11. Pray ten Hail Marys and one Glory Be.

8. Think about the third mystery. Pray the Lord's Prayer.

7. Pray ten Hail Marys and one Glory Be.

12. Think about the fifth mystery. Pray the Lord's Prayer.

5. Pray ten Hail Marys and one Glory Be.

6. Think about the second mystery. Pray the Lord's Prayer.

4. Think about the first mystery. Pray the Lord's Prayer.

13. Pray ten Hail Marys and one Glory Be.

3. Pray three Hail Marys and one Glory Be.

2. Pray the Lord's Prayer.

14. Pray the Sign of the Cross.

1. Pray the Sign of the Cross and the Apostles' Creed.

Mysteries of the Rosary

When we pray the Rosary, we reflect on mysteries or special events in the lives of Jesus and Mary. Mary is Jesus' mother and our mother—the Mother of the Church. When we pray the Rosary, we walk with Mary through certain events in Jesus' life. Some of the events are happy, some are exciting, and others are sad, just as events in our lives are.

The Church has traditionally used three sets of mysteries—the Joyful, Sorrowful, and Glorious Mysteries. In 2002 Pope John Paul II instituted the first changes to the Rosary in nearly 500 years. John Paul added a fourth set of mysteries, called the Mysteries of Light or the Luminous Mysteries, to the Rosary. These new mysteries focus on the public life of Jesus. They include his baptism, his first miracle, his proclamation of the Kingdom of God, and the institution of the Eucharist.

According to the suggestion of Pope John Paul II, the four sets of mysteries might be prayed on the following days:

~ the Joyful Mysteries on Monday and Saturday,

~ the Sorrowful Mysteries on Tuesday and Friday,

~ the Glorious Mysteries on Wednesday and Sunday,

~ the Luminous Mysteries on Thursday.

Praying the Rosary is encouraged as a daily prayer practice. The Rosary can be prayed individually, with our families, or communally with larger groups of Church family members.

We celebrate the Feast of Our Lady of the Rosary on October 7. Praying the Rosary is especially encouraged during the month of October.

The Joyful Mysteries

1. The Annunciation

Mary learns that she has been chosen to be the mother of Jesus.

2. The Visitation

Mary visits Elizabeth, who tells her that she will always be remembered.

3. The Nativity

Jesus is born in a stable in Bethlehem.

4. The Presentation

Mary and Joseph take the infant Jesus to the Temple to present him to God.

5. The Finding of Jesus in the Temple

Jesus is found in the Temple, discussing his faith with the teachers.

The Mysteries of Light

1. The Baptism of Jesus in the River Jordan
God proclaims that Jesus is his beloved Son.

2. The Wedding Feast at Cana
At Mary's request, Jesus performs his first miracle.

3. The Proclamation of the Kingdom of God
Jesus calls all to conversion and service to the Kingdom.

4. The Transfiguration of Jesus
Jesus is revealed in glory to Peter, James, and John.

5. The Institution of the Eucharist
Jesus offers his Body and Blood at the Last Supper.

The Sorrowful Mysteries

1. The Agony in the Garden

Jesus prays in the Garden of Gethsemane on the night before he dies.

2. The Scourging at the Pillar

Jesus is beaten with whips.

3. The Crowning with Thorns

Jesus is mocked and crowned with thorns.

4. The Carrying of the Cross

Jesus carries the cross on which he will be crucified.

5. The Crucifixion

Jesus is nailed to the cross and dies.

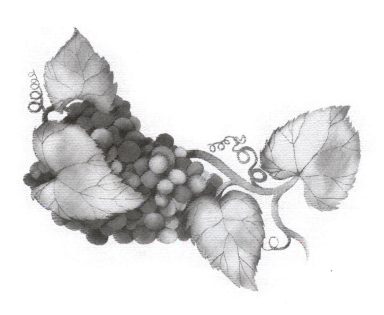

The Glorious Mysteries
1. The Resurrection
God the Father raises Jesus from the dead.

2. The Ascension
Jesus returns to his Father in heaven.

3. The Coming of the Holy Spirit
The Holy Spirit comes to bring new life to the disciples.

4. The Assumption of Mary
At the end of her life on earth, Mary is taken body and soul into heaven.

5. The Coronation of Mary
Mary is crowned as Queen of Heaven and Earth.

Stations of the Cross

As Christians we are called to follow Jesus. The Stations of the Cross represent events from Jesus' Passion, Death, and Resurrection. After Jesus' Ascension into heaven, early Christians used to visit Jerusalem, where Jesus died, to walk in his footsteps. They stopped at different places along the way to think about what had happened to Jesus. They marked the places where they stopped so that others could follow. These places became the Stations of the Cross.

The road that Jesus walked in Jerusalem is today called the Via Dolorosa, the way of pain. When Christianity spread throughout the world, shrines or stations were erected in other places, especially in Europe, for people to remember Christ's Passion. The Franciscans popularized the devotion we know as the Stations of the Cross. In the 17th century, churches placed stations around the walls to commemorate these events.

Just as the early Christians did, we pray the Stations of the Cross to remember all that Jesus did for us. We can pray the stations individually and as a family. Sometimes parishes schedule times for services to pray the stations communally, especially during the Lenten season.

At each station we pause, using our senses and imaginations to reflect prayerfully on the scene or event depicted or described. We can pray in our own words as we reflect on each station, or we can pray prayers written by various people throughout the centuries. Some of these beautiful prayers are provided for us in Stations of the Cross prayer books. No matter how we pray the Stations of the Cross, we focus on Jesus' suffering, Death, and Resurrection in order to deepen our commitment to follow him.

If your church has the Stations of the Cross along its walls or elsewhere, plan a visit with your child to talk together about what is happening in each one. Talk with your child about following the road that Jesus walked when he died for us. Involve your child in a reflection and prayer about each station. For example, when looking at the First Station, ask your child what Pilate might be thinking, what others might be doing, and what Jesus is doing. Relate the scene to your child's life by inviting him or her to share a personal experience that the scene reminds them of. Pray together to Jesus, thanking him and asking his help in being like him.

For very young children, you may want to precede a church visit with the reading of a children's book about the stations, such as *The Story of the Cross: The Stations of the Cross for Children* by Mary Joslin (Chicago: Loyola Press, 2002).

1. Jesus Is Condemned to Death.

Pontius Pilate condemns Jesus to death.

2. Jesus Takes Up His Cross.

Jesus willingly accepts and patiently bears his cross.

3. Jesus Falls the First Time.

Weakened by torments and by loss of blood, Jesus falls beneath his cross.

4. Jesus Meets His Sorrowful Mother.

Jesus meets his mother, Mary, who is filled with grief.

5. Simon of Cyrene Helps Jesus Carry the Cross.

Soldiers force Simon of Cyrene to carry the cross.

6. Veronica Wipes the Face of Jesus.

Veronica steps through the crowd to wipe the face of Jesus.

7. Jesus Falls a Second Time.

Jesus falls beneath the weight of the cross a second time.

8. Jesus Meets the Women of Jerusalem.

Jesus tells the women not to weep for him, but for themselves and for their children.

9. Jesus Falls the Third Time.

Weakened almost to the point of death, Jesus falls a third time.

10. Jesus Is Stripped of His Garments.

The soldiers strip Jesus of his garments, treating him as a common criminal.

11. Jesus Is Nailed to the Cross.

Jesus' hands and feet are nailed to the cross.

12. Jesus Dies on the Cross.

After suffering greatly on the cross, Jesus bows his head and dies.

13. Jesus Is Taken Down From the Cross.

The lifeless body of Jesus is tenderly placed in the arms of Mary, his mother.

14. Jesus Is Laid in the Tomb.

Jesus' disciples place his body in the tomb.

Sometimes a 15th station is included that reflects on the joy of the Resurrection of Jesus.